Jesus said: 'I am the Way, t

GO,
KNOW,
LIVE

A presentation of the Christian faith for young people

Anders Åkerlund and Michael Proctor

SCM Press Ltd Bloomsbury Street London

Design: Michael Harvey and John Salsbury

334 01556 1
First Published 1970
by SCM Press Ltd
56 Bloomsbury Street London WC1
© SCM Press Ltd 1970
Printed in Great Britain by
The Whitefriars Press Ltd. London and Tonbridge

Preface

This is an attempt to present the Christian faith from an ecumenical viewpoint and in a pupil-centred way. The aim is not to give ready-made answers, but to present some facts and encourage the pupils to find their own answers.

Most of the material appeared first in the Swedish book *Jag är vägen, sanningen och livet,* published by Swensson and Åkerlund. We are grateful to many people and organizations for material and advice. We want especially to thank John Bowden, Editor of the SCM Press, and John Hull, Lecturer in Education at Birmingham University, for help with the text, and Michael Harvey and John Salsbury for their attractive presentation.

Selly Oak,
Birmingham,
October 1969   Anders Åkerlund   Michael Proctor

ACKNOWLEDGEMENTS

We are grateful to the following for permission to
reproduce illustrations:

Barnaby's Picture Library, 50, 61; Roy Brody, 39;
Camera Press, 36, 38, 49, 59, 61; Christian Aid, 49;
Graham Jeffrey and Wolfe Publishing Co. Ltd., 15, 19;
Keystone Press Agency, 43; *Methodist Recorder,* 37;
Mirabelle, 47; Noble & Samson Ltd., 59; Rehab, 61;
Shelter, 61; *TV Times,* 5; United Nations, 9;
Valentine, 48.

Believing

PISCES (*February 19 to March 20*)
Your popularity is at its peak, so you will be able to make new friends and acquaintances, some of whom will be valuable contacts in the future.

ARIES (*March 21 to April 20*)
A loved one will suggest an idea which will prove to be worth while for you both, if you act quickly.

Most people like *music* of one kind or another. It is a way of expressing feelings and thoughts. Of course, there are many different kinds of music. What kind do you like best of all?

_____

_____

If you listen to a piece of music, you can understand it in different ways. You can just enjoy the sound, or you can go into it more deeply. You can analyse the technique. You can admire the players. You can be caught by the rhythm, and so on.

What is most important to you when you listen?

_____

_____

We can look at religion, to begin with, in the same way. Most people believe. To believe is to look at the world in a particular way. Just as there are different ways of understanding music, so too there are different ways of understanding the world. These ways are called religions. Give some examples of different religions:

_____

_____

Religions are concerned not only with what we see and know around us, but also with what is beyond. Religious questions are questions like: Where do I come from? What is the meaning of my life? What happens after death?

Our ancestors put weapons and food in their graves: Why do you think they did that?

_____

_____

In some cultures dead people are put in a curled up position as if they were in a womb, because they are believed to be born again to eternal life.

People are always interested in themselves. One popular belief today is in horoscopes. But that is a very impersonal kind of belief.

In the majority of places in the world today and throughout human history, people have looked out beyond themselves to someone above themselves. They have thought that there must be a God. Why do you think that this feeling is so common?

_____

_____

CHRISTIAN BELIEVING

Christians believe that God has shown himself above all in Jesus Christ.

Jesus Christ challenged the world by saying: 'I am the way, the truth and the life.' During this course we shall try to understand why Jesus said this and what he meant. All kinds of people, from statesmen and professors to simple ordinary people, devote themselves to a life as Christians, each in their own way. As you read this book, you will come to understand something about Christianity, too. In your own way, just as you listen to music in your own way.

Of course, there are people who are intolerant of other people's views about music — and you are likely to meet even greater intolerance if you take your religion seriously. What you are going to believe, no-one knows yet. You can come and see what it is about openly and freely. Later on, you can decide for yourself whether or not you want to be a real Christian. Write down frankly why you have begun this course:

_____

_____

(When you finish the course, compare your thoughts then with what you have written here.)

GO The ways to knowledge

THE CHURCH

The building in which you worship

Find a picture of your local church and stick it in here.

Draw a plan of it here, complete with furniture, and label the important parts.

# of God and contact with Him

Either draw or make a list of the things you would need in your church for

1. A Holy Communion Service   2. A Baptism

Your church is not the only one in your area. What other churches are there?

In most churches you will find a priest or a minister. There are various titles for him. Can you name some?

What is the title of your minister?

In this book we are just going to use the word 'minister' to cover them all. Do you know what 'minister' means?

Did you know that churches sometimes advertise in the local paper? Find an advertisement and stick it in here.

The church exists for all men. It consists of all those who recognize that they belong to Christ. We go out into the world to do his work and we come together to worship. There is a place reserved for you every time there is a service, even if the place is empty.

The church exists for all men. But you become a member of the church through baptism.
Are you baptized?

Many people are baptized as babies. Their parents and friends have found such strength and happiness in the family of the church that they want the baby to grow up in that family and share its life, from the earliest possible moment. But the baby is too young to understand his responsibilities and privileges as a member of the church. His parents and the church must undertake to explain them to him as he grows older and to help him to grow up as a Christian. When he feels ready and able, he may be confirmed in his membership of the church and shoulder the responsibilities himself. Many other people are baptized as adults. For them, baptism marks the time when, having learned what it means to belong to Christ's church, they are ready to make their own personal decision to leave their old life behind and follow Jesus Christ.

Either way you can see that we think baptism is important.

Why are we baptized?

Because
Jesus commanded it (Read Matthew 28.18-20)

Because
The New Testament church practised it (Look up Acts 10; 8.26-38; 2.37-42; 16.25-34)

Because
Christians have always been baptized ever since.

So what does it mean for us now?

What does it give us and what does it ask of us?

1. We get a new parent. Who?

_____

_____

Everyone who has ever lived is a child of God. But through baptism we enter into a special relationship with him and we recognize that he is our Father.

2. We get a new family. Which?

_____

_____

Every family looks after its members, especially the younger ones. Every congregation has a special responsibility towards newly-baptized members. Give some examples of how it should be shown.

_____

_____

WHAT WE GIVE
In a happy family all members, young or old, trust each other. The family means something to them and they are willing to contribute to the life of the family as much as they can.

So baptism requires a response from you. It requires a determination to try to do what is best for your heavenly Father, for the other members and for yourself.

All this means that when we are baptized we start a new kind of life. We become members of God's family.

Projects

1. Talk together in your group about infant baptism and adult baptism.
2. Choose a hymn suitable for a baptism and find a prayer (or make one up) to go with it.

Keeping in touch with God

Have you ever said any prayers?

_____

If so, what kind of things do you pray about?

_____

_____

_____

Do you use mostly your own words, or prayers that
you have heard or read?

_____

_____

You have probably at least made a beginning at some
time or another.

People all over the world and of all different religions
say prayers, each in their own way. And you must find
your own way.

We all need to think about certain things that make
all the difference between 'good' prayer and 'bad'
prayer. Good prayer is always changing and growing,
because it is the communication between two living
beings — God and you.

If a friendship is to stay alive, both people must
love enough to take some trouble over it. God takes
care — but you also owe it to him to take care. You
sometimes hear of a family where no-one has taken any
trouble — and so they have all lost contact with each
other. All they say to each other is 'Give me some
more money', or 'Where are my socks?', or 'I'm going
out'. And when they leave home they never bother to
write. If one of them needs the support of the family
it just isn't there. We need the support of our spiritual
family very much and especially of our Father. So in
our friendship with him it is a good thing to set aside
a special time each day for him, then our friendship
will always grow stronger.

Here are some guides which may help you to find your own patterns of prayer.

WHERE?
Wherever you want. In the bus, at school, at home, on a walk. One building is specially intended for prayers and quietness. Which?

_____

_____

Drop in now and then even if it isn't a regular service.

WHEN?
Whenever there is an opportunity. Different for different people. But it is important to have some rules. What could happen if you only prayed when you felt like it?

_____

_____

_____

A habit of regular prayers is very useful. What time during the day would suit you?

_____

HOW?
You can use written prayers or your own words. Don't make it too complicated. God doesn't care much about your English. You can speak as simply and naturally as you can to a good friend.

Write in your own words a prayer about peace and justice in the world.

_____

_____

_____

_____

_____

_____

_____

_____

_____

This diagram shows some of the things you will want to include in your prayers. Why do you think it is usual to close your eyes, bend your head and to put your hands together when you pray?

Confess
Thank
Praise
We
Pray for others
Ask for ourselves

Is God asleep?

Does God notice everything we pray about and everything that happens in the world? Yes. God has promised to hear everything as a good father listens to his children. But sometimes it would not be good if we got what we asked for. Give examples of prayers which would lead to misery if they were fulfilled:

_____

It is also true that God is not the only power in the universe. A lot of evil things happen which are not the will of God. But through the life of prayer we are on God's side.

Praying means being near GOD, THE FATHER OF THE UNIVERSE. It will not free us from troubles, doubts etc. But we may come to him exactly as we are and we can trust in him and know that he loves us.

'OUR FATHER'
There are situations when you would like to pray but you lack the words. This happens to most people. It happened even to Christ's disciples. What did one of them say in Luke 11.1?

_____

Which prayer were the disciples told to use?

'Our Father Wheel'   Fill in what's missing.

GROUPWORK
Divide up the prayer in the group. Try to illustrate it by collecting pictures and giving them captions. Mount the whole project as a collage. You will need to think carefully what each phrase means.
For instance:

1. Why do we say 'our Father'?

_____

2. How can God's name be hallowed?

_____

3. Name something characteristic of the kingdom of God:

_____

4. Name something which you think may be God's will for you to do today:

_____

5. It doesn't say **my** bread but **our daily** bread. What does it mean?

_____

6. Give examples of 'trespasses':

_____

7. Why is temptation dangerous to us?

_____

8. What do you think is the greatest evil?

_____

How will God show his power completely to us? Read II Peter 3.8-13.

_____

Look up what A and Ω mean. Revelation 21.6

_____

Instead of doing it in a group, you could yourself find a picture for each part of the wheel and stick them on a separate sheet of paper.

Some useful prayers

IN THE MORNING

Father in heaven, thank you for the new day which
you have given me. I thank you because it is you who
created me, so I am your work and I belong to you.
Thank you, because my life is in your hands, and you
make my heart beat and my brains work.
Lord, help me to use this day rightly, because you
gave it to me.
Bless all its hours.
Bless all its duties and work, its rest and joy.
Bless the work of my hands, the words of my lips, and
the thoughts of my brain.
Let me live this day before your face and to your
glory.

IN THE EVENING

Father and friend
I commend this day to you.
I thank you for the many good things I have enjoyed:
for food and drink,
for the fellowship of family and friends,
for things achieved and hopes fulfilled ....
I admit to many failures too .... and I ask for
your forgiveness.
And now, Father, I commit myself, and all my loved
ones to your care...
And may the love of the Lord Jesus Christ ever keep
me close to you. Amen.

Use the rest of this page and the one opposite to make a collection of famous prayers of all ages and of different
religions. Don't forget to put the name and religion of the author, and the date, if you can find it.

Some famous prayers

Intercessions

Intercessions are very important prayers in which we bring other people and their needs to God.
On this page make a record in words or pictures of some of the needs of people in the world today.

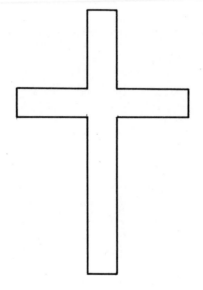

Don't neglect your Prayer Life !

The Bible

The are 66 books in the Bible. They were all written at different times and in different places over a period of thousands of years. They were slowly gathered together until we have them all in one book. It has been translated into 1250 languages, and more are added each year. Generations of men have searched its pages and tried to understand it.
Many books have been written about it.
Is it really worth all this effort? Is it worth reading?

You could read it as a valuable document of cultural history. You could read it as a treasure-house of Jewish lore and customs. You could read it as the world's best collection of poetry and literature of all kinds.
   But, in the first place, the Bible is a tool in the hand of God, to help man to find a meaning to life, and a solution to life's problems:
Where he comes from, why he lives, and HOW he should live; so **Yes: It's worth reading:**

Islanders in Bible Rush

THE PEOPLE **of the little island of Réunion in the Indian Ocean have had their first chance to buy Bibles.**
   Mr. David Cohen, as Bible Society Secretary, had record sales on a visit. In a period of 12 weeks, he sold a total of 12,575 Scriptures, including 1,493 Bibles, 1,251 Testaments, 9,596 Portions and 235 Selections.

ABORIGINAL VERSION

It may be the computer age but primitive languages still survive and modern Bible translation is constantly being applied to them. For instance, eleven teams of linguists are working on translations into 30 Australian aboriginal dialects.

'Have you anything by the same author?'

The Old Testament

In the ancient world, long before Christ, the Jewish religion brought men nearer to understanding God than any other. Jews saw themselves as specially chosen by God, to know him in a special way, and they saw their whole history as being in his hands. They treasured the writing of many great men of different ages — history, laws, prophecy, stories, poems, songs, folklore — which they felt helped them to know something about God. We still keep that great library — in our Old Testament.

BUT we believe that Jesus Christ shows us more about God than anyone or anything else. So why bother with the Old Testament?

Because Jesus Christ was a Jew and was brought up against the background of the old Jewish Scriptures. We can't really understand him unless we know a little about his background.

Here is one way of thinking about the Old Testament and the New Testament: This picture has a greyish background, with a bright face in the middle. The Old Testament lightened the darkness of the world a little bit, then into this greyish background came **Jesus Christ, the Light of the World**. The Old Testament points forwards to Christ's coming and prepares the way for him.

If you look up the passages below, you will meet just a handful of the great men of the Old Testament, you will see how the Jews were aware of God working in their history and you will perhaps understand how their great thinkers came to look forward more and more to the coming of Christ.

ABRAHAM

The father of the nation. Read how God called him away from his family to found a new people.

Genesis 12.1-3

MOSES

The great leader who freed Abraham's descendants from slavery in Egypt, made them a nation and gave them a code of laws. Read how through him God created a special relationship with the new nation.

Exodus 19.1-6

DAVID

The great King of Israel, and their greatest hero. Read the promise that God made to him about his descendants.

II Samuel 7.1-16

ISAIAH

A book of prophecy written by at least three different men at different times. Read how the first of these great thinkers foretells the coming of a mighty king, and how long afterwards another 'Isaiah' begins to understand that this will be a very strange king indeed.

Isaiah 9.2-7; Isaiah 53

There are things in the Old Testament which we find strange, or that we cannot accept at all (look up, for example, Leviticus 11 and Psalm 137.7-9). We have to remember that these writings are thousands of years old and stand at the beginning of our knowledge of God. We may often see in them principles which still hold good. But the main importance of the Old Testament is as a framework within which to understand the teaching of Christ.

The New Testament

In the New Testament we see God's will for men much more clearly, especially in the person of Jesus. So it is very important to study it carefully. If it is TRUE that Jesus Christ is the Son of God — God in human shape — and that the New Testament is an authentic record of his life and teaching, it must be the most important book in the world.

The Good News We have four different accounts of the Gospel ('good news') of Jesus' life and work, his death and resurrection, all of them based on the witness of close friends who had shared his life and work. We can see in these accounts the perfect example of Jesus' life and teaching clearly set out.

Each version looks at Jesus Christ in a different light. No one account could do justice to so great and complex a character. Even with the four accounts we cannot expect to understand him fully.

The Gospel accounts assure us of Christ's victory over sin and death, and so promise us a new freedom and fulness of life. There are differences between the four versions, but then we challenge you to find four people in the crowd at Wembley who would give you exactly the same version of the Cup Final — especially if you asked them about it many years later. (The Gospels were written down long after the events — until then the news had been passed on by word of mouth.) All four assert without doubt that Jesus rose victoriously from the dead, and that we share his victory.

THE ACTS

What happened to the disciples after Jesus left them? The book of their 'acts' gives us an exciting account of the spread of the faith throughout the civilized world. Read for example: Chapter 2; 9.1-30; 19.23-41.

THE LETTERS

Were written by several readers of the young church (notably Paul) and contain advice, encouragement and teaching, sometimes to a particular group of Christians, sometimes to one person, sometimes to everyone. e.g.

Encouragement to a persecuted church   *I Peter 1.3-9*

A rocket for Christians who were quarrelling and dividing into sects   *I Cor. 3.2-7*

Explanation of the faith   *Rom. 5.6-11*

Pleading for love between Christians   *Eph. 4.1-6*

Pleading with a Christian master on behalf of his runaway slave   *Philemon*

THE REVELATION

The last book in the Bible is a very difficult book to understand. It is a vision of heaven expressed through complicated allegory, and in beautiful language. Read Chapter 21.1-7.

It is important for us all to read the Bible and try to understand it. There are several new translations which make the Bible easier to read: New English Bible, Jerusalem Bible, Revised Standard Version and others. And here are some aids that you might find useful:

Scripture Union
5, Wigmore Street, W.1

B.R.F.
148, Buckingham Palace Road S.W.1

Alan Dale
New World (Published by Oxford University Press)

Ask your group leader or minister about them.

The Bible is not an ornament. It is a tool

The Church's Year

The church helps us to understand the meaning of Christianity and to grow in our Christian life by following the events of Christ's life, Sunday by Sunday.

The old couple were going to church. A raw, rainy evening and the old woman said to her husband: 'Today let's go to church and get some consolation in the word of God. And I'd quite enjoy a good old sing.' The old man muttered but went with her. Afterwards he was angry. 'What did I say? Dark and dull. The minister only talked about sin and judgement and they sang depressing hymns.' They had happened to come on the first Sunday in Lent. Look up the Bible readings for that day. What are they about?

If the couple had come six weeks later, everything would have been different. White colours, preaching and hymns joyful and happy. What Sunday?

The church's year can be divided into two parts, centred upon Christmas and Easter.

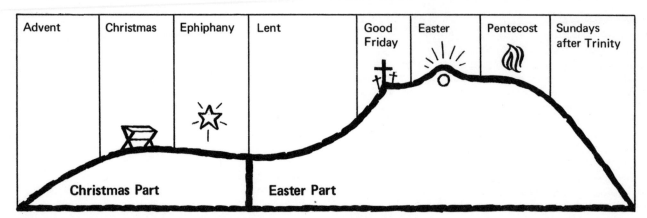

The church year also changes like the life of a man.

Fill in the names of the Sundays.

Themes	Sundays
Before birth	
Birth	
Joy, thankfulness	
Sorrow, passion and death	
Resurrection	
Life	

Some churches use different colours to stress the meaning of the day.
Each part begins with a time of preparation.

Violet is the colour for repentance and preparation.
The climax is A GREAT FESTIVAL.
White is the colour for joy and festival.
This is followed by the GROWING TIME.
Green is the colour for the growing of faith.
Red is the colour for the Holy Spirit and the martyrs.
Black is the colour for sorrow and judgement.
Why, then, is the colour for Easter Sunday white?

What happens when the family comes together?

On this page set down the pattern of the service that you normally attend.

_____
_____
_____
_____
_____
_____
_____
_____
_____
_____
_____
_____
_____
_____
_____
_____
_____
_____
_____
_____
_____
_____
_____

In this column use some symbols to show what you are doing at each point in the service, e.g. Standing – !, Sitting – = Kneeling – Z, Speaking – " ", Singing – δ etc. And mark the parts of the service which seem most important to you.

That's what happens—on the surface

But have you grasped what really happens?

Family worship

Life and worship go together
If you are alive you worship
When you worship you really come alive

Why is it important for the family to come together?

1. CONTACT

No man is an island. We need contact with each other. We need to share both troubles and joys.

We have contact with God in our prayers, singing and listening. We share our joys and troubles with him too.

2. KNOWLEDGE

The family benefits from coming together, because we learn about ourselves and each other.

God gives us his word in the Bible readings and in the sermon. We gain knowledge about him and about ourselves through the scriptures and the experience of others.

3. TRUST

Confidence in each other binds the whole family together. We speak frankly with each other. This should also happen in God's family.

In our worship we learn to trust God and we learn also that he trusts us. We speak frankly with God in confession. God gives us his forgiveness.

4. FELLOWSHIP

The family meal is the centre of the family fellowship. Round the table we really become ONE family.

God gives himself to us in the bread and the wine. We give ourselves to him and to each other in our renewed determination to go out and live our lives in his service and the service of others.

Christians worship in many different ways, but next time you go to church, listen and watch carefully and you will find all these ingredients in the service. Some of the time we are learning about God. Part of the time we think especially about other people. We also declare our trust in God, we admit how untrustworthy we have been, and yet we hear how God is still ready to trust us. Sometimes, too, we all take part in a great act of fellowship and remembrance, just as Jesus asked his disciples to do.

In worship we use words, music, silence and actions to remind us of our closeness to God, and our duty in the world. Try now to think critically about the services in your church. You might like to discuss them in your group.

1. Is there enough silence in the service? Or enough action?
2. What do you like most/least about it?
3. There are many new forms being tried out. Is your church trying one? What are the differences and why do you think the changes have been made?

Your service

Write down the different parts of your service in the appropriate boxes

1. CONTACT

2. KNOWLEDGE

3. TRUST

4. FELLOWSHIP

The most important service is the **EUCHARIST**.

Why is it celebrated?
When Jesus was on the earth he had his disciples and also other people around him. In the inner circle they shared everything, and they had their meals together. In the time of Jesus, eating together meant much more than it usually does to us. By eating with someone you showed that you accepted him as a very good friend.
What happened according to Luke 19.1-10?

_____

_____

How did the people react?

_____

Why?

_____

_____

_____

When Jesus knew that he was soon to be killed and to leave his followers, he asked them to remember him in the sharing of bread and wine. Then when he finally left the realm of time and space, his followers knew that he was still with them, even though they could not see him, and they were especially reminded of his presence in the Eucharist.

The Eucharist was founded during the Jewish passover. Why was the passover celebrated? Read Exodus 12.1-14 In this way Christ filled old traditions with a new meaning.

The meaning of Eucharist

LIBERATION
Passover was celebrated by the Jews in remembrance of the liberation from the slavery in Egypt for us Christians, the Eucharist brings liberation from every burden and strain. Give some examples.

_____

_____

_____

_____

_____

THANKSGIVING
Find out what the word 'Eucharist' means. What language is it?

_____

_____

What can you thank God for in the service?

_____

_____

_____

FELLOWSHIP
In the **Eucharist** we can experience a close fellowship with God in a special way. Christ has promised to be with us every time. We may also believe, that we are so near the eternal God, that the frontiers of time and space disappear. We can know that we belong together with all Christians in the whole world and of all times. That's why it is called HOLY COMMUNION.
What communion?

_____

_____

_____

REMEMBRANCE
In the Eucharist we remember what Christ has done for us. He reveals himself to us. Read Luke 24.13-34. When did the disciples recognize Jesus?

_____

_____

_____

_____

Did you know that bread and wine was poor man's food? Many poor people in our world today live on wine and bread only. They can be seen sitting in the

street, eating a little to survive. It is typical of God's action among mankind to use this simple method of communicating with us. Christ used the poor man's daily food to establish a deep contact between the creator of the universe and his children around the world.

Read I Corinthians 11.23-25. What words are used about the bread?

_____

What words are used about the wine?

_____

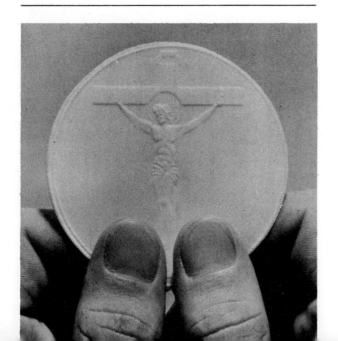

IT IS GIVEN FOR YOU!
The family meal is the centre of family life. Each one of us has a place in that fellowship.

If God himself bothers to look for us, how can we just shrug our shoulders and neglect him ?

Helping

To live, and to live as a Christian, can be a very difficult task to do on your own. But why on your own? We are here to help each other. We can help each other in many ways, both material and spiritual. But the minister can help us in a special way if we want to use him. He is used to most situations. Nothing can really shock him. You can speak quite freely and without pretence. Nothing will leak out. He is bound to silence over confidences. Nor will he seek to judge you himself.

To fall short, to fail, to feel guilt, these things are common to all men. The minister can be a safety valve to people with problems. He is ready to listen to you. Don't be afraid to speak out when it's needed. Make contact before it's too late. The mind is a sensitive instrument, not to be played with or neglected.

In counselling (or confession) and in the church services and prayers, we can hold up our failings and sins before God. We Christians know that we may throw everything like that away on God, and he forgives us everything. This means that we may begin again and again with a clean sheet, and leave all the old rubbish behind us. So we can be open and free people.

Some churches use sacramental confession. This usually consists of three things.

1. Counselling with a minister
2. Confession before God.
3. Absolution. That is, the minister tells you, as a message from Our Father, that you are forgiven.

The minister is the dustbin of the congregation. He is also there for you and your problems. Don't be afraid to disturb him. He has become a minister just to be of service. He has the authority of Christ to tell people of God's forgiveness.

Write the name of your minister here:

List other people in the parish who help

KNOW

So far we have talked mostly about the way to Christian life. Now we shall talk a bit more about what Christians believe. We shall use the Apostles' Creed as a basis for our discussion.

I believe in God

the Father almighty,

Maker of heaven and earth:

and in Jesus Christ

his only Son our Lord,

who was conceived by the Holy Ghost,

born of the Virgin Mary,

suffered under Pontius Pilate,

was crucified, dead and buried,

he descended into hell;

the third day he rose again from the dead,

he ascended into heaven,

and sitteth on the right hand of God the Father almighty;

from thence he shall come to judge the quick and the dead.

I believe in the Holy Ghost;

the holy catholic church;

the communion of saints;

the forgiveness of sins;

the resurrection of the body,

and the life everlasting.

The creed consists of four parts: I believe in God, the Father, the Son and the Holy Ghost.
First let us try to see the relation between the four parts of the creed.

1. The men of the Old Testament times and Jesus worshipped God.
2. They came to think of him as the Father of all mankind.
3. The first Christians began to understand that Jesus was more than an ordinary man — they began to worship him as God.
4. But they still felt the presence of God with them after Jesus had left them. They called this the Holy Spirit.

This DOES NOT MEAN that we worship three Gods — but one in three. We use a special word to describe this — **Trinity**.

The Trinity

Our God is one, but he is three. What can this mean?
Our whole existence is complicated. We can see this
from modern science. If our religion was simple, we
would probably think that it was an over-simplification.
But our religion is complicated, like the world as a
whole. There are parallels to the doctrine of the
Trinity in nature. They can help us to understand.

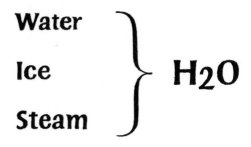

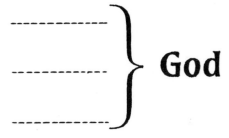

Fill in on the dotted lines.

A triangle is a good symbol for God.
One God but three forms.

God

All religions bear witness that there is a God. What does does the Bible say about who GOD is? Look at the following passages, and write one or two words about each of their pictures of God.

Isaiah   40.9-17

_____

_____

_____

Psalm   46

_____

_____

John   1.18

_____

_____

_____

Matthew   5.48

_____

_____

_____

I Corinthians   13.10-12

_____

_____

_____

I John   4.8

_____

_____

_____

_____

Our human intelligence is too small for us fully to understand God. We can only talk about him in picture language — and God is too great for our pictures. He is the underlying power in the universe. He is behind everything that is good, and he is present in every situation.

BUT WHERE IS GOD?

Some people think that God is somewhere 'out there' at a certain place in space. But that cannot be true. In Australia, you know, they pray 'downwards' while we in Europe pray 'upwards'! When we pray towards 'heaven' it doesn't mean that God is only there. God does not live on a special cloud somewhere. But it is a sign of humility before the great God to think of him as 'above' us.

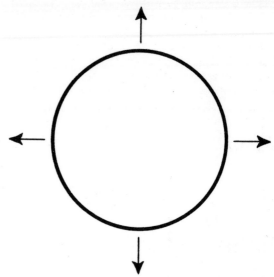

We are used to thinking of things in terms of **space** (in a certain place), of **time** (e.g. April 24th 1969) and of **cause.** For example: You are sitting in a particular room (space) just now (time). That you exist depends on God giving you life through your parents (cause). The Bible says that this is not true of God. He is different from us. He is:
independent of space = he is everywhere,
independent of time = he is eternal,
without cause = he is not created. He was from the beginning.

It sounds perhaps peculiar, but everything must be possible for God, who could create the world.

How can we answer when our non-Christian friends say 'Where is God?'
Discuss it in your group.

The Father

Through Christ that great God threw his titles away to be close to mankind. In Hebrew the word father is 'abba', the same as our 'daddy'. It is a familiar word that expresses intimacy. There are many who unfortunately have real hooligans as parents. God is not that sort of father. Since we may call God 'daddy', it shows a close relationship. Sometimes people have been afraid of God. Sometimes even parents use God to frighten their children.

Christ has taught us to feel confidence in God. He is a loving God who wants us to feel safe by his presence in our life.

Can all this and much more have been developed only by chance? We who write this don't think so.

What do you think?

The Creator

Go out into the countryside on a fine day.
Tense your muscles and feel how you can control your body.

Think what powers we advanced people have among ourselves.

'And just look at His use of colour in the left-hand corner!'

People have always been wondering where everything has come from. They feel that someone must be behind it. An eternal God, who created our world.
Read the creation story in Genesis 1.1-2.3 carefully.

Who created the world?

_____

_____

_____

What did God think of what he had done?

_____

_____

_____

_____

_____

_____

What was created last?

_____

_____

_____

_____

Name some details which are not in accord with modern science:

_____

_____

_____

_____

Do you think that you have to believe in the details literally to be a real Christian?

_____

_____

_____

You may not be able to see what this picture is, nor what it means. It is not an exact photographic image of what the artist sees, but rather an expression of his personal feelings and experience. But we must still accept that his art is real. The creation story is an artistic drama trying to express the great and incomprehensible creation drama. It says simply that God created the world and that he had a good purpose for it.

For discussion

What can the story teach us that modern science cannot?

Sustainer

God didn't just start everything and then leave it. He goes on supporting and maintaining his creation today. He stands for righteousness, life, goodness, etc. Look up the following passages and write them here:

Psalm 95.4

_____

_____

_____

John 5.17

_____

_____

_____

_____

_____

He's got the whole world in his hand.
He's got the whole wide world in his hand.
He's got the whole world in his hand.
He's got the whole wide world in his hand.

    He's got you and me, brother, in his hand.
    He's got you and me, sister, in his hand.
    He's got you and me, brother, in his hand.
    He's got the whole wide world in his hand.

He's got everybody here in his hand.
He's got everybody here in his hand.
He's got everybody here in his hand.
He's got the whole wide world in his hand.

Almighty

God has power. But he doesn't use his power against our will. He didn't create us as computers programmed by someone behind the scene. We have our free will. God didn't make us as creatures who can only obey without thinking. He wanted man to be mature and be his partner.

Everything that happens isn't God's will. There is also an evil power, that tries to destroy God's plan for mankind. Sometimes people have thought about it in a very childish way as a kind of monster, e.g. with green face, horns and tail. If it was that simple then we could

How dead is the Devil?

get it in a corner and kill it. But the evil power is more complicated than that. Even in the church, through history the evil power has worked quite happily.

Give examples of the frustration of God's power in the world today.
And in the church.

_____

_____

Can you see the power of God working anywhere now?

_____

_____

As we can see, there is a fight between God and the evil power. When will we finally see that God has the greater power?

_____

_____

_____

Jesus Christ

JESUS CHRIST WAS A REAL MAN
How do we know? If you want some help see for instance Matthew 21.18; John 19.28; Matthew 26.36-39.

Jesus was his name: Christ is a title, 'anointed', 'Messiah', which he is given. 'Christians' means 'followers of Christ'.

Jesus was trained in a trade. Which? See Mark 6.3.

___

No-one knows what Jesus looks like. But he has made a great impact on every age since he lived on earth. Artists have tried to present their understanding of him in different ways.

He Lived. A historical fact. Jesus is no fairy tale. He really existed. Different kinds of ancient writings talk about him.

A Roman historian: '. . . . Christ, whom Pontius Pilate had condemned to death during the rule of Caesar Tiberius' (Tacitus, about AD 100).

An opponent of Christianity at the time: 'Jesus has done sorcery and seduced Israel and made it turn from God' (Curse formula about AD 100).

New Testament: 'Jesus from Nazareth . . . walked around and did good things and cured everyone' (Sermon by Peter, about AD 40).

He lived here and he made quite an impression!

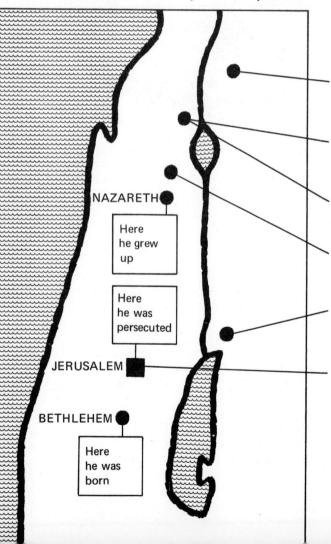

NAZARETH

Here
he grew
up

Here
he was
persecuted

JERUSALEM

BETHLEHEM

Here
he was
born

These people met him. There must have been something special about Jesus. Some became his followers, some his enemies. No-one could be indifferent to him.

Simon Peter:
'We believe and understand that you are God's holy one'.

Roman officer:
'Lord, I am not worthy, that you should come under my roof'.

Pharisees:
'This man receives sinners and eats with them'.

Mary:
'Whatever he tells you, do'.

John the Baptist:
'Look, the lamb of God that takes away the sins of the world'.

Commanding officer in charge of the crucifixion:
'Surely, he was the Son of God'.

If we think only of Jesus' life on earth he offers us no hope. Even by human standards he seems a failure.

When a noble son of a king is born you would expect splendour and homage. At the birth of Jesus it was quite different. Compare and fill in the dotted lines:

What you could expect	How it was according to the Gospel
Courtiers	An Ox
Maids of honour	A Donkey
Castle	
Bed	
Rich parents	
Married parents	
Comfortable mattress	
Beautiful clothes	
Homage of distinguished people	

Jesus was later executed as a criminal. Read Luke 23. 32-43. Who were executed at the same time?

_____

_____

_____

The question is, how something that happened nearly 2000 years ago can have such an importance now, that people even today can gladly devote their lives to it.

If Jesus' life on earth had stopped at the crucifixion, he would have been helpless among helpless people. But it isn't so. **Jesus** came to liberate the world and give us a new hope, new freedom and a new fighting spirit. How? Jesus is not only a real man but also a real God. He is Lord of all things.

But we talked about God as almighty before. How could he let his own Son be killed on a cross by men?

A great church leader once wrote: 'The almighty made himself helpless because of his love for us'. These words tell us why **Jesus** had to suffer. God didn't want to leave us alone; instead he came and shared our human conditions. He was one of us. He was not afraid to live simply and to give himself to others. He was even a helpless child. He lived as a poor man among poor people, just as most of the people in our world have to live today.

Nothing human can be unfamiliar to Jesus. Because of that everyone can see himself, his situation and his problems in Jesus. He came to share our situation completely. He came for you and me.

Jesus Christ was a real man

But he came to bring the power of God into our situation. How can you see this in the Gospels? For your help, look for instance at Matthew 9.35; John 11.39-44; Mark 2.1-12.

_____

_____

_____

He shows us God's power most clearly in his resurrection from the dead. That is God's great challenge to all evil. The resurrection of Jesus shows that there is a victory and a triumph even over death. Read I Corinthians 15.3-9. To whom did Christ show himself after the resurrection?

_____

_____

_____

Many people think that faith in Christ risen from the death is a delusion and far too incredible. Opinion stands against opinion. Many others think that if Jesus really was God he was able to destroy the power of death. Furthermore: What happened to the disciples who hid like frightened chickens in a house in Jerusalem after Christ's crucifixion but very soon afterwards stood up bravely and bore witness to the risen Lord Jesus Christ? And later on, most of the eyewitnesses died as martyrs. It is even more incredible that they made up the whole story. No-one would die for a bluff.

We cannot scientifically prove whether the resurrection is true or not. You must decide for yourself if you dare to believe it or not. But here are some reasons for believing that the resurrection really happened.

He is living now

You can meet him. Jesus is no longer dead. He is alive again. He is with us at all times and in all countries. He himself said: 'I shall not leave you without a father. I shall come to you.' 'Where two or three are gathered in my name I am in their midst.' 'I am with you till the end of the world.' You can recognize him in worship, in the meeting of Christian people and in many places besides. Perhaps not all at once, but later on. He is waiting for you.

Conclusion

Christ underwent the deepest humiliation, took all the problems and guilt of men on himself and won a victory even over death. Therefore we don't have to fear anything. Christ wants to free us from all evil to inspire us to courageous and open living. He is on our side. Who can be against us?

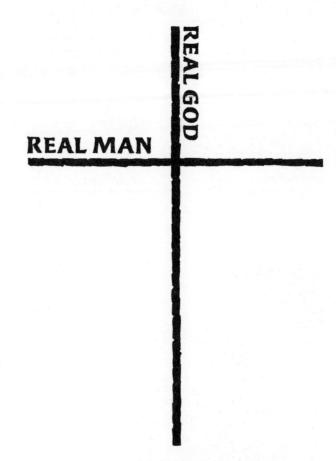

REAL GOD

REAL MAN

Jesus Christ Real God, Real Man

Compare the two pictures of Christ given on this page. They are rather different. Describe the differences.

_____

_____

_____

_____

How do you imagine Christ?

_____

_____

_____

_____

You might like to make a collection of pictures and sayings which show how people of different ages have understood Christ.

REWARD

FOR INFORMATION LEADING TO THE ARREST OF

JESUS CHRIST

WANTED

for revolt and sedition, criminal anarchy, contempt, disturbing the peace, leading a riotous assembly, subversive activities, etc.
Simply, almost shabbily dressed. Said to be a carpenter.
Suffering from malnutrition, and visionary delusions.
Commonly consorts with casual workers, unemployed, tramps, and prostitutes.
Of foreign, probably Jewish, extraction.
Alias: The King of Peace, Son of Man, The Light of the world, etc.
'Mods in West Berlin'

The Holy Spirit

The first Christians felt the presence of God still with them after Christ had left them. Read Acts 2.1-4. The Holy Spirit is often called the helper. When faith grows and blossoms, that is the work of the Holy Spirit. He is God's working hands in his workshop — the church. Look back to page 20. If you compare that page with this, you may see where the Holy Spirit comes in.

1. KNOWLEDGE
Many say that they don't dare believe in God. To be able to believe, you must know a little at least of what he stands for. An Indian boy learns from his father to understand the language of nature. If the sun goes down in clouds it will probably rain tomorrow. Rain is good for hunting. He must gain knowledge by experience. And so it must be in more and more profound things.

2. CONTACT
It isn't likely that you could become a Christian and understand religious reality by yourself. You must have some help to see it. Behind that prowess is the Holy Spirit. In this course you have the opportunity to begin to live with a Christian faith.

3. FELLOWSHIP
You can leave everything to someone you trust. Even troubles, doubts and questions. The church offers fellowship with God and other people.

4. TRUST
A weather cock changes direction with the wind. Many people live like weather cocks. They are very uncertain, don't dare to stand for anything and only follow the crowd. They have no backbone to their lives. They lack maturity.

God is the creator and lord of the universe. He wants to support us and give us that backbone and maturity. All these are marks of the spirit.

Where God's spirit really is, you can find joy, openness and enthusiasm. It works against resentment and unwarranted pessimism. It also works to develop your character. What should be the Christian attitude? See Galatians 1. 5.22-33 and Corinthians 13.

But the Holy Spirit is not only confined to the church. Do you remember the liturgical colour of the Holy Spirit? If not we are not going to tell you. Look on page 18.

It is also the colour of revolution:

These men think they are something.

(And in some respect they are).

Who are they?

But they are peanuts before God.

Look up Revelation 21.5 and see God's purpose for the world.

God is not static. He is developing the world. You can never stand still in your human and Christian development. It is true that God is the God of order, but he is also the God of change and renewal.

God is the greatest revolutionary of all time

The Church is One

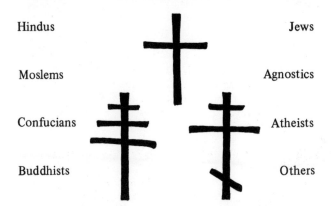

Hindus	Jews
Moslems	Agnostics
Confucians	Atheists
Buddhists	Others

Every third man on earth is baptized and a member of a Christian church. The others belong to other religions or are outside religion. In every country there are Christian churches. In the creed we do not confess a faith in the church organization or the buildings. **We believe in the church**, the invisible unity of all Christians, the world church.

DIVISION
During the course of history the churches have become divided for various reasons. For example:

1. Different opinions about baptism, the church, Holy Communion, salvation. Can you give an example?

_____

2. Historical and political reasons. Can you give an example?

_____

3. Personal reasons: Can you give an example?

_____

Division always weakens.

UNITY
Christ said: 'I pray that they may all be one'. His life was a fight for unity between God and mankind, between man and man. Unity is needed for our mission. Otherwise the non-Christian world will not take us seriously. Why?

More and more Christians see the need for unity. They know that division is against the will of God.

ECUMENISM
(i.e. the work for the inhabited world = Greek Oikoumene) is the name of the movement that aims to unite all Christians.

WORLD COUNCIL OF CHURCHES (WCC)
Is a fellowship of Orthodox, Anglican and Protestant churches and movements. It is not a government over the churches, but a platform for co-operation and mutual understanding. It studies questions about unity and our responsibilities in the world. It co-ordinates practical work for people around the world. In each country they have committees. In Britain it is represented by the **British Council of Churches** which inspires Christian co-operation in many fields. It has an increasing importance.

'We shall get nowhere with this unity business if you keep asking me what I mean!'

For discussion

1. Why is the church split?
2. Is it necessary for the church to be united? If so, why?
3. Is there a local council of churches in your area? Why? (or Why not?).

The Church is Holy

The church belongs to a Holy God. Through baptism the members belong to God. God gives us the forgiveness of sins and the Holy Spirit teaches us to be more and more like God.

When we say that the church is holy, we mean the universal, invisible church. Traditions, forms and organizations you have a right and perhaps even a duty to criticize. The church as an organization is not without failure. The church cannot stand still. It is and must be a living organism. That's why the members are so important. Your task is to make it a living church, fighting fit in the modern world.

The apostle Paul talks about Christians as holy. In this context it means that we belong to God. Unfortunately it does not mean that we are not sinful. Naturally every Christian must strive to be less and less sinful. This is called holiness. We follow Christ and try to imitate his love in our lives. To be a Christian means never to settle down and be satisfied as a man. It means to move and develop. Read Colossians 1.10. What does it suggest to you?

_____

_____

_____

For discussion

Is it necessary to criticize and develop the church?

The Church is Catholic

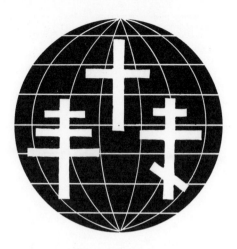

'The church is catholic' means that it is for the whole world. That is an immense task. Without people like you, we cannot manage. The church is for everybody. Who was welcomed in Luke 15.7?

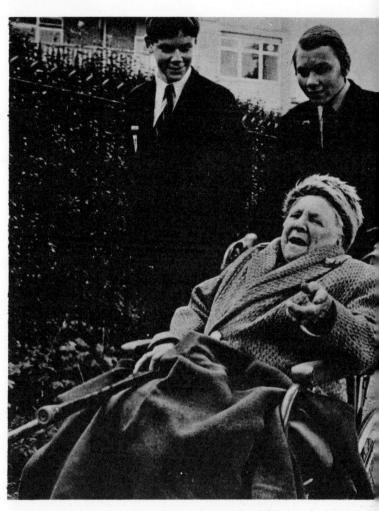

God wants everybody to be saved. (I Timothy 2.4). Jesus preached, and so does the church. Jesus helped ill and distressed people and the church is trying to do the same. The two missions of the church HERE and ABROAD are in reality the same.

Christ is the first world-citizen. He wants to destroy all discriminating walls between people. What walls, for instance? See Galatians 3.28.

A believer asked a young man what he expected in life.
He answered: 'First I want to take my 'A' levels and go to a university'.

And then?
Then I want to get a well paid job, buy a detached house, relax and enjoy myself.
And then?
Then I want to marry and have some nice children.
And then?
Then I want to make a career and to be something.
And then?
Then I will be old and become a pensioner.
And then?
Yes—I'll die in the end (he said, hesitating).
And then?
I don't usually think about it.

Why are people afraid to think about death?

We don't like to think about what happens after death. We try to escape from it. In the Victorian age it was taboo to talk about sex. Now it is equally horrifying to talk about death.

But a Christian can believe that we have eternal life. God didn't create us like disposable containers to be used once. We are complicated and precious creatures and God has promised never to throw us away. He is stronger than death.

That's why we can believe in an eternal life. Not because it is especially reasonable.
In what ways has God showed that he is stronger than death?

_____

_____

What will happen when we die? We don't know much about it. But some things we know. Read Matthew 23.31-46.

_____

_____

What does 'resurrection of the body' mean? How do you think we can rise? See I Corinthians 15.42-44.

_____

_____

What can we be sure of when we die? Read Romans 8.38-39.

_____

The Resurrection

Illustrate the life of man according to this story with some pictures on the next two pages.

of the Body and Everlasting Life

More space for illustrations

LIVE

THE RULES OF LIFE

Traffic regulations. Are they necessary? For instance, you have to drive on the right on the Continent and on the left in Britain. Such rules protect both our lives and those of others. What would happen if we had no rules to guide the traffic?

Rules of Life are necessary to protect and develop life. The ten commandments are in Exodus 20.1-19. If you don't know them, look them up and fill in the dotted lines below.

THE TEN COMMANDMENTS

1. You shall have _____ but me.

2. You shall not make yourself any graven _____

3. You shall not take the _____ your God in vain.

4. Remember to keep holy the _____

5. Honour your _____ and your _____

6. You shall do no _____

7. You shall not commit _____

8. You shall not _____

9. You shall not bear _____ against your neighbour.

10. You shall not covet your neighbour's house, you shall not covet your neighbour's _____ , nor his _____ , nor his _____ , nor his _____ , nor his _____ , nor anything that _____

As you can see, the ten commandments talk to a particular time in history. It was a time when worship of images was common. It was a patriarchal time when the husband nearly owned his wife like a slave, for example. But still the commandments are meaningful to us. In what way, we shall see on the next pages.

Notice that the ten commandments are not the same for every church. Many have dropped the second in the scheme above and divided the tenth in two.

The Ten Commandments

Two headlamps light up the road when you drive in the dark. You can see the edge of the ditch, holes, curves and pedestrians. You can steer the car and save lives and avoid disaster.

The two tablets of the law had the same function. Their contents are summed up by Jesus in Mark 12.30-31. Look it up and fill the dotted lines.

You shall love

_____

_____

_____

_____

And you shall love

_____

_____

_____

_____

God has made the world. He gave us our conscience, an instrument that tells us that we shall do this or that. We must always keep our conscience in touch with the will of God, especially as we find it in the New Testament — otherwise it is easy not to hear it!

The First Tablet of the Law

You shall love the Lord your God.

First Commandment
You shall have no other gods but me. No other gods. God is our best friend. Nothing can be more important than him. You cannot gamble your life on success only, nor can you have fellowhip with money. We give our hearts to God.

Second Commandment
You shall not make yourself any graven image. This commandment was given to prevent people from leaving God and worshipping other gods. We have seen that God counts on you and me in his plan for the world. We give God our loyalty.

Third Commandment
You shall not take the name of the Lord your God in vain. Honour God's name everywhere. At home, among friends, at school, in church. We give God our prayers and witness.

Fourth Commandment
Remember to keep holy the sabbath day. Be careful with your Sundays. They are a double gift, at least for those who are free from work.
(a) Meet God. Don't miss the opportunity.
(b) Relax from work and duties. We give our time to God.
1/7 of your days are Sundays.
What do you make of them?
Make a timetable for a Sunday, with time for both yourself and for God.

Time	Activity

The Second Tablet of the Law

What commandments?

You shall love your neighbour as yourself.

To love yourself

To love your neighbour

Neighbour = The nearest
At home?   At school?   Among your friends?
In the street?   In life?   In the world?

(Fill the coil from the middle)

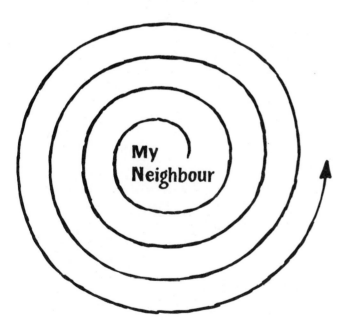

My Neighbour

Commandments 5 and 7 talk about home, love and the family.

Fifth Commandment
Honour your father and your mother. Home and Family

You will never get out more than you put in. We are all responsible for our home.

1.   What can parents do?

(a) _____

(b) _____

(c) _____

What can young people do?

(a) _____

(b) _____

(c) _____

Compare and discuss your answers with others.

Supposing that you are to have children of your own, how would you want them to be brought up?

1. More freely?   2. More strictly?

3. As you have been brought up yourself?

There once was a boy who liked to go to church every Sunday. But his parents didn't approve of it and teased him. They said: 'What is there to do there? That's a lot of old rubbish. You ought to stay at home instead.' What do you think that boy should do?

_____

_____

Something similar happened to Jesus, too. When? Try to remember the story. If you can't, look up Luke 2.41-50. What happened?

_____

_____

_____

The ABC of Love

Seventh Commandment
You shall not commit adultery. What does 'adultery'
mean? Nearly every human being has a desire to be
loved by someone of the opposite sex and to be
intimate with her/him. Many are disappointed for
various reasons. Can you mention some?

_____

_____

_____

_____

_____

_____

Among animals love life seems to be less complicated.
They often have a special time for sex according to the
time of the year, their age, climate and so on. We are
ready for sex biologically quite early, but not mature
enough to take care of the product of love — children.
To have children too early provides a lot of serious
problems. Name some:

_____

_____

_____

_____

_____

Often we can see a difference between the sexes too.
Girls want to be romantic and tender with their boy-
friends and are not ready for intercourse and advanced
petting. Boys seem to be more straightforward and
often try to take what they can get. They sometimes
look for intercourse to show themselves and their
mates that they are 'real men'. But often it's an idle
boast and in reality they lack experience.

In many countries you will find pornography teasing
the curiosity of man. It often creates a fanciful world
full of sex and aggression that cannot be healthy for a
natural and successful sexual life. Perhaps we have so
many cheap, erotic books and magazines because we
lack real and true love.

SOME RULES FOR DISCUSSION

1. Other people are not for your enjoyment.
Christian love asks you not merely to take but to
give.

Many people eat their meals like animals. You cannot treat people in the same way. They ought to be
the object of our care, not means to our own enjoyment. Many boys talk, for instance, about girls who let
them do what they want to. What do you call such
girls?   It's seldom that those boys are interested
in them as personalities. These girls often try to be
popular but in most cases they lose their own and
other's respect.

2. To break something always hurts. The Bible says
that you become one flesh with someone through
intercourse. That means a deep fellowship. A grown-up
man has often the opportunity to plan his life in
advance. He is less flexible than a youth. He is more
tenacious and more stable. As a youth you can change
plans and desires as you like. Even if you are abso-
lutely crazy about someone today you may probably
lose your interest after less than a month. So don't go
too far. You will probably regret it. You must be free.

3. Some modern prophets of sex preach that it is
the with-it thing to sleep with as many people as possible. What's so revolutionary about that? The most
with-it thing is to have some self-discipline — and so
become a truly mature person.

4. The Church looks at sexual love in a positive way.
God has given us this gift to express a deep fellowship
with another person and to have children by it if we
want them. So the church doesn't want us to bring it
down to a selfish level. In order not to destroy this
method of communication it is much better to save it
for the person that you are willing to share your
whole life with. (In a matrimonial relationship intercourse can give joy to both people and deep communion in a relaxed feeling of security.) The best
advice you can take is to wait for that situation.

What do you think about these rules?

How and why can it be wonderful to be together with a boy/girl?

_____

_____

Can it be frightening, if so how?

_____

_____

Try to give your answer to the following letters:

I am just 15 and I have fallen in love with a wonderful man. The only trouble is that he is a lot older than I am, and he is already married. He says he loves me very much and when I ask him what about his wife, he just says she can look after herself. I don't know what to do. I know my Mum and Dad would be furious if they found out, but I can't bear to give him up.

_____

_____

All my friends go out with boys and have a good time, but although I desperately want a boyfriend I just don't know how to go about it. I'm beginning to think there is something wrong with me . . . . I'm 14 and I think I'm quite attractive.

_____

_____

_____

Some time ago a friend told me she had seen my boyfriend out with another girl, and when I asked him about it he said that there was nothing in it and he promised to stop going with her. Now I discover that he is still seeing her. What shall I do? I think I'd die if I lost him.

_____

_____

_____

My boyfriend always wants to go a lot farther than I do. He says that if I don't give in to him it means that I don't really love him. I'm desperately afraid that if I don't give in he may leave me.

_____

_____

TOGETHERNESS

JUST being together with Tim meant something new . . . something wonderful for Susan. But it meant something frightening, too . . .

LOOK AT THE PICTURE

Do you think a marriage like this could be successful?

Try to explain your answer.

_____

_____

_____

_____

_____

_____

_____

What qualities would you look for in your future husband/wife?

1. _____

2. _____

3. _____

4. _____

5. _____

What do you think you have to do to make your marriage successful?

1. _____

2. _____

3. _____

4. _____

5. _____

Before you marry, think if you want her/him to be the mother/father of your children.

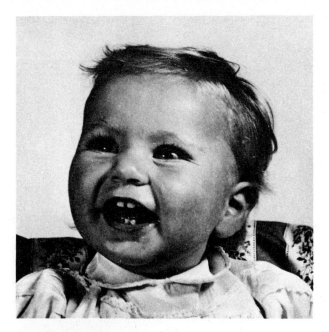

How much is a life worth?

Sixth Commandment
You shall not kill. Unborn, but with the right to live.
Most of us have a high standard of living. But we may
think that there is not room for more children to be
born. Instead of that we destroy the unborn child, 'it's
the cheapest way' for the society. It is called abortion.

In some respects this is an exaggeration. Sometimes
an abortion can be necessary. When?

_____

_____

_____

When do you think that life begins?   Explain:

_____

_____

_____

An unmarried mother is depressed. No housing. No
money. No chance of taking responsibility for the child.
How can society help her?

_____

_____

_____

_____

_____

£3 a month for life

This Chinese boy has a future through foreign aid for only
£3 a month. He has been able to go to school. He wants
to learn as much as possible to be able to help in the
development of his community.
A very small part of our national income goes to aid
developing countries. Do you think that we can give
more? Are you willing to give something? _____ s
month.

£130,000 for a dead man

Every dead enemy in Vietnam costs the U.S.A.
£130,000. Research in Washington produced these
figures. Compare them with the amount of money for
keeping a man alive and giving him education. See
above.

Try to make some suggestions how we as individuals
can develop a new kind of thinking, to share a greater
part of what we have with the have-nots here and
abroad.

But they gave as good as they got!

Organized murder = War

We are living in a cosmopolitan age. We ought to have an increasing understanding between people and nations. Why can our time be called cosmopolitan? Name two serious tension points in the world today:

_____

Many still think that violence and war is tough and manly. What is the peacemaker called in Matthew 5.9? The beginning of violence is aggression in our inner life. It's important to do something about that too.

War must be considered as something evil and against the will of God. But sometimes you may have to commit a sin in order to prevent a greater and even more disastrous sin. Can you think of any situation when war is fair and right?

Respect what belongs to others

Eighth Commandment
You shall not steal. The breaking of the eighth commandment is a big problem in society today in many ways. Name some of them:

_____
_____
_____
_____
_____
_____
_____
_____
_____
_____
_____

Ninth Commandment
You shall not bear false witness against you neighbour.
Man has: 2 eyes to see with. 2 ears to listen with. 2 nostrils to smell with. But only 1 mouth to speak with. Conclusion: You can tell only half of what you see, hear and smell.
Make this double examination of what you say. Ask yourself.
1. Is it true?
2. Can it hurt anyone?

Always sift your words carefully

Tenth Commandment
You shall not covet your neighbour's house and so on. Every magazine and paper that you read is full of advertisements. These may not be bad in themselves, but they could lead us to break the tenth commandment if we are not careful.

Collect some advertisements on the next page and try to explain how they might tempt people to covet.

Advertisements

Two lights from a car light up a dark road. It is natural and useful to use them. But are they enough for a safe journey? What else is needed?

The two tablets of the law try to light up the road of life. Many agree that it is natural to keep them. But is it enough to know what you should do? Why do we not keep them always?

1. The commandments are not an escalator to God. We cannot earn his grace. But they are useful for our guidance.
2. They protect life and righteousness and hinder the growth of sin.
3. They show us what we are like inside, just as a mirror shows us what we are like outside.

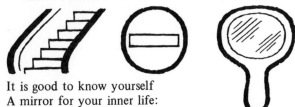

It is good to know yourself
A mirror for your inner life:

Question: In what way have I failed to fulfil the will of God?

TOWARDS GOD:
In thought:

In word:

In deed:

TOWARDS MY NEIGHBOUR:
In thought:

In word:

In deed:

Often we feel like St. Paul. He had the same problem. See Romans 7. The evil that makes me fail God and my neighbour = Sin.

God sent his own Son in the world to take our sins and failures on himself, to encourage us through his example, to give us inspiration and to save us from our vicious circle.

Salvation means that we are made free by God. We can be forgiven for everything. We can always start again. Our life may be completely in God's care and full of his blessing.

This is my world

Collect some pictures or short stories on these two pages showing our situation in a welfare state.

But…

It might have been this

Get some pictures or articles which show some facts about the need of the world today.
Put them on these two pages.

ONE CAN REACT TO DIFFERENT SITUATIONS # Like this . . . . . .

Stick some pictures here which show our lack of awareness and our lack of action over the suffering in the world.

or like this . . . . .

CHRISTIAN 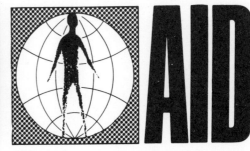 AID

Where does Christian Aid send aid?

_____

_____

_____

How much does it need each year?

_____

_____

_____

When is Christian Aid week?

_____

_____

_____

**Five new pence –
or it might be**

A bar of chocolate   15 mugs of milk in Hong Kong
a soft drink   a visit to the clinic in Jordan
a Sunday paper   a text-book in Ethiopia

Which shall it be?

or like this . . . . .

Jesus said 'He who would be greatest among you must be the servant of all' (Mark 10.44).

OVERSEAS

1. Which missionary society does your church support?

_____

2. How many missionaries does it maintain?

_____

3. Where are they?

_____

4. How much does it cost to keep the work going for a year?

_____

5. How much for a second?
   Can you spare a second?

_____

Put crosses on this map to show where missionaries from your church are working.

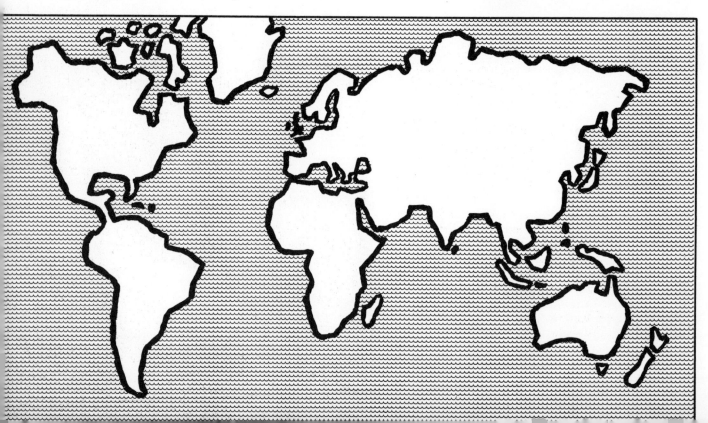

HELP! Look around..

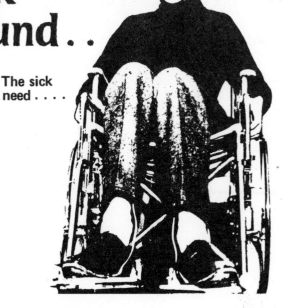

The homeless need . . . .

The sick need . . . .

LOOK AROUND
Who needs what round your way?
And what can you do about it?

The lonely need . . . .

The elderly need . . . .

THE YOUNG NEED . . . . ACTION!

Look up Matthew 25.31-46. Read it together in your group and then discuss it. What was Jesus getting at? Does this passage make any demands on you?

What do you give?

THE BRICK

The bricklayer laid a brick on the bed of cement.
Then, with a precise stroke of his trowel spread
another layer.
And without a by-your-leave, laid another brick.
The foundations grew visibly,
The building rose, tall and strong, to shelter men.
I thought, Lord, of that brick buried in the darkness at
the base of the building.

   No one sees it, but it accomplishes its task, and the
other bricks need it. Lord, what difference whether I
am on the roof-top or in the foundation of your
building, as long as I stand faithfully at the right place?

From Michel Quoist, *Prayers of Life,* published by
Gill and Son, 50 Upper O'Connell Street, Dublin,
Ireland.

QUESTIONS:

Why are the ordinary Christians so important for the
Christian church?

_____

_____

_____

How can you in practice become a living 'brick' in the
building of the church in the world?

_____

_____

_____

Pray for power to realize such a life. God trusts you
and he needs you. You are included in his great plan of
the world.

   Write some names, perhaps the names of your friends
in your study group, on the different bricks of the
church. You, together with millions of people in the
world, are the world's church-building.
Perhaps you are wanted by God as a pastor/minister
for instance??????

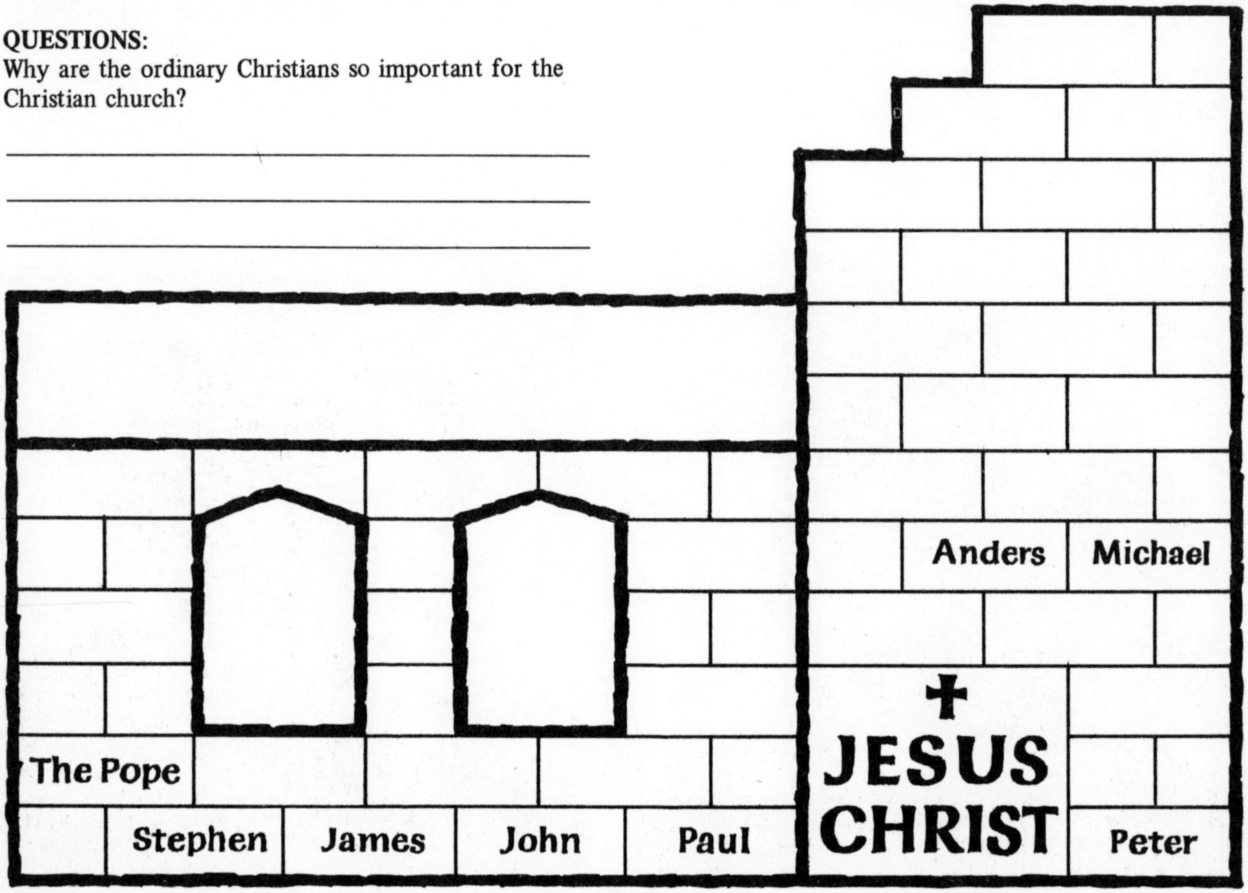

What do you get?

We have now briefly covered the topics of the Christian faith, but it is a good idea to go over them again now, and from time to time in the future, so you never forget them.

Your character and personality will develop a lot during you life. **Please give your faith a chance to develop too.**

Otherwise you will soon come to reject it as many middle-aged people have — thinking it is childish and naive. What they in fact throw away is often their childish idea of Christianity — but they have nothing to put in its place. Please keep your faith up-to-date.

Try to summarize the Christian gospel under the heading:

Why I want to be a Christian

_____
_____
_____
_____
_____

Compare this with what you wrote on the first page.

Write down something that is hard to understand and something you have doubts about.

_____
_____

You can still be a Christian even if you have such doubts on your mind. It is impossible to understand everything now and even ministers have doubts about certain things. St. Paul says: 'Now we see only in part, but then we shall see face to face.'

If you want, you can discuss it with your teacher. If you have read this, you must know that you are loved by God. But God doesn't interfere in a domineering way in your life. You have the freedom to say 'yes' or 'no' to God's offer to become a follower. Now God has tossed the ball into your court. It depends mostly on you how your life will be.

Someone asked an apostle in the Bible if Christ had anything to give. He answered, 'Come and see'.
Jesus said: 'I am the way, the truth and the life'.
Jesus said: 'I am the light of the world. He who follows me shall not walk in the darkness, but shall have the light of life.'

We hope that you will join us on the road. God bless you.